Telling Gestures

Joy Pitman

Chapman Publications
1993

Published by
Chapman
4 Broughton Place
Edinburgh EH1 3RX
Scotland

The publisher acknowledges the financial assistance of the
Scottish Arts Council in the publication of this volume.

A catalogue record for this volume is
available from the British Library.
ISBN 0-906772-46-X
Chapman New Writing Series
Editor Joy Hendry
ISSN 0953-5306

Some of these poems have previously appeared in:

Fresh Oceans (Stramullion), *Hens in the Hay* (Stramullion),
Original Prints II (Polygon); *Chapman, Graffiti, Northlight,
Pages, Radical Scotland* and *Spare Rib*

Designed & typeset by Peter Cudmore
Cover design by Fred Crayk

Printed by
Mayfair Printers
Print House
William Street
Sunderland
Tyne and Wear

Contents

Introduction

Telling Gestures

Contents (*continued*)

Introduction

Joy Pitman's poems work almost subliminally, creeping up on you with their intensity, their emotional charge, the exuberance of their experience, their simmering sexuality. These are not poems of the particular. She is a writer who deals in moods, sensations, relationships, the verities of nature, the diurnal round. The people she writes about seem to live on the edge of the five senses which fuse, fly, fall in dramatic dances. They connect, circle circumspectly, make love, drift apart, chill into silence. Few contemporary poets have written so well about non-communication as Joy Pitman. A poem like 'Silence' eloquently expresses how, when lovers drift apart, words dry up and "waves of anxiety spin out". There is pain in every line.

Such sentiments are rooted outside time, like Jane Austin. Joy Pitman rarely furnishes her poetry with references to contemporary events: she prefers classical allusion to news footage, using myth, fairy tales, ineradicable rhythms, diamond-hard words, to reinterpret modern dilemmas, age-old perplexities.

Nature dominates these poems, as in deed she must, providing the impetus, the energy, even violence, as in the poem titled 'May', where the poet speaks of the "power" of blossom "to rouse and stir me", of the "ferocity" of spring which can rip "the life out of my belly". As the earth is affected so too is the poet who feels a similar sensation in the presence of a lover:

> Just as your beauty
> Can seize me by the throat
> And rack me with a joy
> Inseparable from anguish.

This is the beauty that Yeats said was terrible but in Joy Pitman's poetry it is also tender and compassionate. These poems are quite fearfully personal but they do not cloy in the manner of *soi-disant* 'confessional' poetry. The poet seems to keep a respectable distance from her material; the language, the lyricism, does not allow her to get too near. The first person is frequently present but while this gives the poems directness the poet is often wrestling with herself, trying to twist logic, to make her centres hold, to involve the reader in her struggle.

Thus, in 'Contradiction', she must consider how, as the

mother of two boys, she has also brought into being two potential killers: "men/ who kill/ in blood/ deal death/ with fear." Or in 'Daddy', a raw series of snapshots bleached of sepia nostalgia, where the poet relives her relationship with her father, an excruciating memoir that evokes child abuse, physical and mental, that makes Sylvia Plath read like nursery rhymes. It takes the breath away with the bleakness of its vision, the brutality of the language.

I don't remember when I first met Joy Pitman. Sometime in the 'seventies, I think. I was working in Edinburgh City Libraries' Reference Library and she was one of those who drifted in and diverted me – it didn't take much – from the incessant enquiries of the general public wanting to know which washing machine to buy or why the latest issue of *Autocar* wasn't on the shelf. Maybe we were introduced by Colin Kerr, the softly-spoken editor of *Graffiti*, where some of the poems in this book first appeared. *Graffiti* has since closed, a sad fact of life for a small magazine. Others, notably *Radical Scotland*, have gone too. Scotland's first feminist publisher, Stramullion, has likewise disappeared. There was even a publishing hiatus at *Spare Rib*, where 'Contradiction' originally surfaced.

But the very mention of the names brings back the era when Scottish writing was beginning to reassert itself after two decades in the doldrums. There were new publishers, writers who mattered, even though a publisher like Virago could only be found in such offstream bookshops as the First of May in Edinburgh's Candlemaker Row.

This is where you were likely to find Joy, at a reading or just browsing. Sometimes I would see her for a coffee or lunch at the Laird's Larder in Victoria Street. Its walls partly decked out, so it was said, in toxic wallpaper that had killed Napoleon. Other times I'd bump into her in the street, sometimes wheeling a bike, always with a heap of books in hand.

She read omnivorously, rapaciously. This is reflected in her poetry – its philosophical toughness, its lightly-worn learning, its wisdom. Her poems reflect clarity of thought, her sure-footed way with technique. Collected they demonstrate that what started as a trickle has over the years built into a dam-burst.

Alan Taylor
May 1993

Telling Gestures

My thanks go to all those who have encouraged and inspired me to keep writing, including the *Hens in the Hay* team and other members of that writers' group; to Joy Hendry, George Byatt, Tessa Ransford, Peter Redgrove and Penelope Shuttle; and especially to Anita Mason, the first to do so, and Gordon Spiers, who still does.

The hunchback in the cellar

The hunchback in the cellar
admits no one but me
I bear a sheaf of ancient papers
their tattered folds too brittle
ever to smooth again
and drifted soot obscures
the marks I sensed in darkness
my fingers are smutted with secrecy
but Quasimodo winks and nods
towards the humming red machine
the rotted cord
breaks with a touch
I trust the magic engine
which charges dust and fixes shadow
to reproduce the hidden images
black spiders' ghosts
against the crisp white sheets

Birth

Within the brown and secret earth
The roots reach down
To find the water's running.
Seeds swell. Bulbs break.
The pale shoot strives into the sun
And greens and buds and blossoms.

So nature flourishes
Although we wound and stunt her
And the ever-present pulse of Spring
Bursts out in leaf and flame.

And here, where true to ancient metaphor,
He's ploughed my furrow, sown his seed,
The child that's fed by flowing blood
Now stirs and quickens
To turn to the uncertain light.

– reminding us,
For all of our cerebral fantasies
And tangled, insignificant emotion,
That even we are of the earth
And dance to ever-beating rhythms.

contradiction

women
giving birth
in blood
dealing life
with love

I have two children

men
who kill
in blood
deal death
with fear

I have two sons

sometimes they play
with guns
sometimes I
hold them

these are contradictions
which carry
like a wound
or a bright red flower
at my centre

May

Along the old canal
A haze of new-leafed green
Is laced upon the silhouettes
Of ash and beech and willow,
While in the park
The almond and the cherry
Burn livid pink on copper,
Freeze white on charcoal brown,
And fill my heart with terror.

For every May the coming of the blossom
Has power to rouse and stir me,
But this year Spring with new ferocity
Has ripped the life out of my belly
And left me gasping wordless cries,
Just as your beauty
Can seize me by the throat
And rack me with a joy
Inseparable from anguish.

Bilberries

Why search for summer's berries
When shoots spring green?
Surrender to this moment
On which the seasons turn,
In time enough
The future draws us
And bitter bilberries
Will ripen.

Lover

Why can't my body be content
To seek that one, or take
This one that's offered
Where I perhaps could ease
This urgent longing?
Why can I find no comfort
In my own care and cunning?

I want to love with head and hands,
In sensuousness find sense,
I want to feel with feeling.

And if our hearts could beat in time,
And if our minds could dance together,
And if our thoughts became entwined,
Why should I not be satisfied?

I want to hear your pulse beneath my fingers,
And taste our limbs entangled.
I want our every sense to sing
The counterpoint of loving.

I want to love with hands and heart,
And see with sensuality
I want to feel with feeling.

lunch

hello
nice to see you

> looking at your eyes
> your hair

eating lunch
and drinking coffee
lighting cigarettes

> noticing your hands
> wanting
> to touch them

exchanging information
fragments
of our lives

> not knowing
> what
> to say

smiling
at your words

> smiling
> at you

well
we must meet again

> my urge
> to kiss you

bye then

> hanging

see you

> in

bye

> the air

fantasy

Each time I fantasise what I might say
I'm sure of your reply
But in reality you won't have learnt
Your lines as well as I.

sales patter

sorry
I don't deal
in parts
this item comes complete
no dis-embodied spirits
and you can't unplug my heart
the body's integral
you'll have to take the package
whole
and by the way
you'll need to treat with care
they haven't worked out yet
a way to make
replacements

Henry Moore's reclining figure – two piece

bronze bulk
upon a pedestal
with holes and spaces
where my children
play and climb and laugh
unmindful of
the Deep Significance
of Art
while my reclining figure
on the grass
thinking of you
ponders the deep significance
of being
one piece

salt in the air

wavelets and eddies
tease
to and fro
early summer shore
barefoot
first shock of water
cold sharp clear
you
excite
my pulsing nerves
invigorate
my pounding blood
there is salt in the air
between
touching us both
I breathe
you meet me
right through
cold sharp clear
I want to wade
your fronds of weed
swim
this sea

dreams of desire

sometimes as I lie
in your warm-limbed easy affection
I have dreams of desire
the potential between us
polarity's call
and your full blood moon
drawing my current
'til this power that grows on resistance
flows out of the ground
and the lightning leaps down
to shock us
to sear and transform

is this the charge
you are laying against me
when you lie
in my easy and warm-limbed affection
do you
ever dream of desire

desire

you pull me
through the whirlwind's eye
up to an icy pinnacle
and spin me round
to hurtle
down the darkness
into the dragon's jaws
which spew me burning
through the desert
gasping for a taste
of your mouth.

Seed

The seed knows the flower,
dreams each petal winter long
folded upon petal,
waits patiently for frozen ground
to ease with weeping showers,
can sense the rolling of the earth
towards the sun.

Love knows already how to bloom,
only requires
acknowledged tears
to thaw the bitterness of need.
Warmth draws her,
unfurling into care,
touch breaks her bud,
desire
opens her in joy.

masquerade

I'm an idiot of verbosity
typecast as the tragedy queen
who fumbles the lines for laughter
and ruins the comedy scene

but a kind-hearted fool came playing
and raised up a ghost of a smile
and taught me with telling gestures
that mime is an eloquent style

for she sensed through my wordy poses
the child in need of the sun
of holiday-treat surprises
and dancing and feasting and fun

she showed me that under the motley
was a body that echoed in need
and you don't have to pierce the patches
to know that harlequins bleed

so I shan't lift the white-faced mask
to see if the jester can weep
for the clown and the poet are one
in loving and dreaming and sleep

Sonnet

Scented by mists from Peruvian peaks
You enter my life a sun-burst surprise,
You tell of a path the wanderer seeks
With suggestions of song in your eyes.
This unconscious ease has opened my heart.
Graceful unwinding warm by the fire,
Words leap between us, we touch and we spark
Unlocking laughter delight and desire.
I want us to dance a ritual Pavan,
Tangle together and roll down the hill,
Drink deep and run barefoot over the sand,
Part again, meet again, do what we will.
I dream of the Cup and the fountain within,
Of the singular sharp salt taste of your skin.

eclipse

sun hangs
relentless zenith

while the dark moon invisible
is riding the sky
moving nearer
spinning closer
gracefully
graciously
to shield the scorched earth
gradually turning
approaching

conjunction

and the force line of their meeting
sucks life blood
tugs blood life
pull gilt excrement
against resistance
against prison bonds
against tight bands
against pangs and pains
in the unending scream of creation

drawing sea tide
neap tide
to cover parched ground
birthing
merciful shadow

and her shining white featured radiant
face to him
full to him
eclipses
his shattering brilliance
covers
his smelted gold

revealing around her

the undulating slow motion spuming
the streaming uncoiling corona
of his potent and burning beauty

the dark moon is visible
high riding the blue
taking
her noon time bright lover

Earth's plea

Lusting for mastery of death, you, in your arrogance,
Have raped my secret depths, forged weapons from my fire,
Blighted my pure breath and poisoned living water.
You render me infertile: my offspring are still-born,
And mind-engendered monsters rise to plague you.
How can I come to you, recoiling from your plunder?
But I your very ground must shake beneath you
To open wide, devouring my despoiler.
The sun will darken, forests rot, crops fail and moulder,
Wild birds fall screaming from the sky;
For you have fouled the sanctuary, excreted in the fountain,
Hurled curses on the wind, blasphemed against the sky;
You plot, you plan, control, rehearse, prevent,
Resist the reach, the leap of spontaneity, refuse the exaltation.
Man, you have engineered your Mother's murder.

Yet do I sue for peace with you
And offer loving terms for your desired surrender.
You may propitiate, appease, weep for your sacrilege
And purify polluted streams with tears of expiation.

Come. Enter me naked, vulnerable, consenting;
Descend the darkness, dare the burial chamber,
Submit to death a willing victim.
Perform the act of sacrifice: for I can heal, make whole.
Your blade will be renewed in my blood-flame
To cut the broiling smoke of senseless machination
And clear the skies for star-shine to illumine you.
Obey my deep-laid laws, flow with my currents,
And I will make my rivers sing in you.
Dance barefoot celebration on my hills,
My earth will thrust her laughter back through you.
Admire me with your crafts, write cunning words for me,
Compose new songs, paint pictures to my beauty.
My fruits will grow for you, my valleys blossom,
My seas will swell their waves against your shore,
My dark and light will beat in every cell of you.
Come, let us set no limits to our love,
And I will live at peace with you.

Elderberry wine

Rich clusters droop into my hand
October light slants mellow;
You lift your pleasure-heavy lids,
My breasts hang glad for you.
Black berries glisten, picking time,
A tongue encircles eager,
I breathe the winter on the air,
And taste your sharpened savour,
There's revel in the autumn leaves,
Bright water dapples golden;
My bowl is generous, weighed with fruit,
A yield that needs be taken.
Let's press the juices of this hour,
Lay down communal wine,
Enjoy, full-bodied and mature,
Our seasonable vintage.

The harvest of my heart is ripe:
Come, meet me now, and gather.

Afternoon in the Botanics

Burst lurid out of dark desire
to break through branching skin
exotic blooms of passion
lie open to the sun.
Love's lily roots in flesh
and from that dissolution
the steady leaves unfurl
the interface of air and water,
the buds make slow explosion into light.
Our bodies lean familiar, touch,
while overhead thrush-throated rhododendrons
sing unabashed with joy.

spinning

lightly
our fingers dance on skin
and subterranean currents flow
we find each other's mouths
and taste a thirst
that breaks from a darker spring
pulled by the tide between us
our bodies rock together
in the surges of the sea
we are both circle and the centre
where the ritual will be

turned on the spindle of our sex
flesh   heart   and mind
merge form
weave colour
spin stars into the sky
whirl out
leap
spark
take meteor flight
fall
gently glowing
where we lie
exhausted
waiting for our dizzy selves to still
and be the same

but we have taken part
in an ancient alchemical rite
subjected our elements
to the vortex of flame
we shall be subtly
but forever
re-arranged

seashell

inside
your seashell spiral
that's ringed with echoes
of the pulsing tide
we meet and melt the edge
of sense and self
you touch me
deep
where feeling centres
and our greeting there
sends ripples out through flesh
dissolving the distinction
between given and received

and with the selfsame movement
fingers of thought
reach down
with care
and taste the salt
of landlocked tears

Danger – thin ice

after each frost
another film
thickens the ice

looks
firm and steady
if
you don't stand
just here
this fine crack
is deceptive
widens
down through the layers
becoming a fissure
a crevasse
a chasm

I'm afraid
of the fall
and the cold
and the dark
icy water
so don't
come
too close
unless you can
hold me
from drowning

eumenides

this one's for me I said
no hesitations this time
no limitations here
I said

not reckoning with
these other ones
inside my head
whose shadow chills me
when I look to you
whose judgements strangle words
and intercept our kisses
their clumsiness confuses tenderness
their expectations
paralyse
so when we try to meet
our scars come in
between

but still we reach
and touch
and touch again
each next time
and the next
untying one by one
the knots
which bind these furies
to the present
until we free them
to the past
where they become
the kindly ones
who heal
the mangled time

peacock

now my lovely peacock
I have seen your richly-spread display
been dazzled by the iridescent turquoise green and gold
admired the splendid crest the fine laced tail
so you can furl your gorgeous feathers
for you will not need them here
I do not want you to parade perform
be do act anything
I am only asking for the present
that we set aside these plumed and painted masks
and curl around each-other through the darkness
our single sparrow selves

fire ^

see this flame I hold in my hands
bright for you
glowing

but if you find the heat
is too intense
I'll cup my fingers together
and set it inside me
safe
in case you should ever
feel cold
and want warming

so come close
let me hold you
and don't be frightened
of burning

Cold

I move and work and talk and laugh
I even dance and sing,
Although inside have a place
That's dark and bare and cold
– an icy stone each morning
That I ache from curling round.

And so you come along with smiles,
You breathe on me, you touch me,
You hold me close and warm me through
"Til I can feel the coldness sharpen,
Fragile against your heat.

And then you turn and cry
You cannot enter there,
For you might recognise
Your own cold places
Where I might burn
Or turn and leave them frozen.

silence

sometimes
your silence grows enormous
fills the room
and drowns
what I have tried to say

waves of anxiety
spin out
from your mute centre
wash over me
and no matter how I grasp
at phrases
they do not reach
the place within the whirlpool
which you cannot name
so any love I offer you
will only batter
against your pain

at times like these
I've tried to stand
some place
a little further off
and give you
something I hope you'll find
acceptable

my silences
for yours

forgive me
all my words

hold me

you hold

me

my love

you hold

off

my love

you hold

me off

my love

Conversation

words words
easy flowing
thicken the air
so I cannot see
tell me a story
and hide what it means

words words words
that ring in my ears
so I cannot hear you
and fill up the space
so we cannot touch

words words   words words

inconsequential design
on a glaring ground
for I see more clearly
between
and the pattern of silence
in sharp relief
loudly declares
that you don't want
anything
to be said

or maybe
you just can't
tell
what you want to say

War Games

1: report from the front lines

"Bravo!" I cry
as I bleed (but don't die)
"you have a most accurate aim"
since I showed you the mark
lined you up to my heart
do you think I've no right to complain?
ah but watch, these firearms are heavy
the recoil they hand out is deadly
you may find it's yourself that you maim

2: non-violence

now dear if you keep fighting
you'll score a hit or two
for I have no urge to carry shields
I'd rather let your weapons through

does that make my love a tactic
or honesty just another game?
well it doesn't really matter
I'm dis-arming just the same

meeting

there was a moment on the hills
when the hare and I
locked eyes
she upright in the heather
poised
with long ears lifted
and nostrils wide to scent me
if I threatened danger
and I unmoving
caught between heartbeats delighted
while the moment
lengthened in stillness
until we heard the hunter's distant gun
and she was gone

and like some brown-eyed creature
unexpectedly encountered
you granted me a moment's meeting
across the space between us
before you turned
and fled

Depression

Wave after wave
brutal and cold
in uneven
yet certain
succession
batter
and submerge me
nightmare screaming
struggling
leave me
gasping
waiting
no pause
the onslaught again.

If this is a shore where the sea recedes
there should be space for resting,
and if the sun would shine a while
perhaps I'd have a chance to grow
to breast the flood
and keep my head above
the next time.

But if the moon should turn
unfavourable
I cannot weather out
another winter solstice.
The neap tide
will drown me.

Five cynical songs

I

Oh you don't want me
I'd be faithful and true,
No you don't want me
I'd demand things of you.

Oh I don't want you
For you can't see
And you wouldn't be true
To yourself or to me.

Oh no I don't want you.
But I want you
To want me
But I want you
But I want
But.

II

I'm disenchanted
midnight's gone
no more dancing
with masked partners
so don't come round
with empty slippers
this Cinderella's going to keep
her feet upon the ground

even if she still enjoys
a fairy-tale at bedtime.

III

Don't worry dear, you've made it clear
You're weary of love's game.
Just keep your mask impassive
I won't insist you play
And when you've cut the last link through
I'll put my heart away.

Now – let's talk of other things.

IV

last season's love
has faded fast
and this year's styles
aren't made to last
sincerity goes out of fashion
and honesty grows thin
so I'll wear my cynicism longer
and tuck my trust well in

V

let's be
carefully
care free

glimpsed

touched on it
didn't we
glimpsed it
I thought
that moment of almost-knowledge
before the dream breaks
the about-to-happen meeting
with the unknown
you thought
that nightmare monsters
were lurking
in the gloom
I thought
I saw a light there
glimmering
well
who's to say
now

unreachable

fist over starving fist
I climb
the braided rope
that issues from my belly
where the greedy navel mouth
devours hungry
every inch I gain
and over me still hangs
unreachable
the vast white moon

Hallowe'en

Blackness thickens.
The silence of others asleep grows palpable
And sets you alone this Night of all nights
When the powers of good lie at ebb of the year
And the tide of evil is rising
To this, the witching hour.
Now all the wandering wraiths from the past,
Every blood-sucking ghoul and bat-winged fear
That's spawned in the dark of the mind
Crowd you close and breathe near
'Til the bony fingers of terror
Come clutch at your throat
There!
Stroke of twelve.
Midnight's here.
You can cross the invisible line
From death into hope,
Into birth, into light.
Day will appear.

Fallow

Last season's fruit is sold
The fields are bare.

And who are you to call me blocked?
Where is your husbandry?

This is the fallow time:
I am tending the earth,
turning my layers of compost,
digging the rich manure
into the waiting ground.

I know these words for seed
and trust Spring winds to blow.

hourglass

emptiness billows
rises dark
out of the vortex
where the white sand
falls
like water
until the moment
when directions spin
the glass
turns
time upon itself
and brightness
stands full measure in me
for the instant
before it runs
away

Labyrinth

I've been in this labyrinth before:
I remember the dark and the cold,
The feeling in my fingers is familiar
When I reach for an answering warmth
And find that there's nothing there,
I recognise the way my words
Are thrown back at me from blankness
And I know you won't reply when I call.
So I shan't shout your name in despair
Or beat with my fists upon dead-ended walls,
I must find my own route down the tunnels,
For my Ariadne was a wise old witch
Who gave me no threads to follow
But taught me to trace back my footsteps
Right into the heart of the maze:
The way in to find out my way here.

PMT: congestive dysmenorrhoea

My breasts have ached all week:
my womb drips words upon the page.

The woman in the desert holds
a dead child in her arms,
her throat is full of sand,
her breasts are empty, dry.

No one has suckled me.
My milk is rancid, festers,
I am turned in.

Black shadow woman,
I will mourn for you,
quarter the round horizon with my cry,
wring tears from scorching air,
descend this grave, devour
the rotting carcass of the child.

The shrivelled crone lies in my arms,
bites through the straining skin
and draws my poison from me.

Above below, we are transposed,
reversed, from inside out.

Her milk is sweet,
she cradles me.

I feel the infant leap within.

full circle

I have passed to the centre
of the maze
gone round full circle
and emerged again

I was not lost

I saw you to the door and said goodnight
put out the light
and turned to face the rising day

and if you say I cried upon your shoulder
– it was at old betrayals
for you have not diminished me

I have gone under
held my breath
surfaced
and breathed again

I did not drown

September

I see how the nightshade hangs
between the rose-hip and hawthorn
while the moorhen who stalks the canal
on the weed-web matting the water
is only a head's turn away
from a comforting rush of death
on the railway line's cold sure steel

but despair is the dark underside
of an urgent lust to be living
and the elderflowers of June
have ripened to purple September
and the fruit of my midsummer days
is distilled and preserved in an image
no lover can carelessly steal away

Ariadne to Theseus

The scarlet cord snakes through my hands
Uncoils the labyrinth
Where groping down the blinded tunnels
Your numb face scents the darkness.

I wait here at the threshold
Remembering the welcome stranger
Who set his key to ingrown locks
And opened for this weary priestess
The unexpected sanctuary above the maze
Where steady candles burn.

Only the monster at the heart
Reveals the dark core of the flame
Enables the rewinding journey,
So I endure your absence
Down the corridors of pain
And spin love's blood thread to its limit.

Penelope

Left to right and right to left
Obedient to a hidden rhythm,
Her fingers blindly count the threads
And draw across the shuttle:
A spark of gold among the blue
May touch another one below,
Relationship as yet unseen
In undecipherable design
Of over under, warp and weft.

The woman who remained behind
Has no more words to greet him;
The warrior who embarked for struggle
Is not the man who might sail home:
His Odyssey is not within her,
The night sea journey still unknown.
But as she works the coded pattern,
Transmitted steady beat by beat,
The mystery in her heart unravels:
This tapestry will be her own.

The "no" she gave her last fond suitor
Defines her borders newly found,
Her body's recognition.
So if a stranger should return
To stand inside her chamber,
To bend the bow they could not master
And shoot his arrows true,
These other selves will find reunion
And different greetings may be spoken:
The sun her love is weaving now
Will shine out then against his ground,
The thread will not be broken.

Merlindene – Fife

Yesterday the world was all one whirling white
sky, sea and shoreline blurred,
distinctions and directions lost.
But now, although the ice still
clings upon the hill tops
where the wind blows bitter,
there's sun upon the dunes
and a skylark rising singing.

This morning when the tide withdrew
the rocks stood dark and naked,
drowning and disaster jaggedly revealed.
But now the waves have covered them
the surface barely ruffled by their presence,
sunlight rippling and the boats away
while sea-birds dive and cry.

I have my own cold peaks and dangerous crags
my own bleak winter
and memories of shipwreck toll in warning,
but in me still thrusts life that will not take denial
a spring indomitable as this.
I may as well leave harbour.

April

I do not know how I can bear
This year
The blossom on the tree.
Dark filigree of twig and branch
Quite barren all the winter
Now feels the force of sap
And bursts brittle skin
To stab me
with their fierce bright colours.
For Spring must come,
Life, love and hope,
However late the frost.

Over Colden Water

Green nimbus pour droplets of water up into the blue
Veined roots cradle their branches puddled in light
Grass stars spark the peat-water sky.

The Hanged Man continues to smile.

Meeting at Colonus

They warned me to expect you
Ancient abandoned child
Self-blinded by pins of guilt:
A sister-daughter leads you here
To stand where the Furies gather.
Our journeys are the same
Back to the womb grave mother.

You entered ignorant the place of issue
Your riddle-solving pride was crowned
The field where you were reaped re-sown:
My labyrinth was threaded to the core
With female love and cunning
To slay fair Ariadne's monstrous brother.
While you took on your father's blood,
Relived in her the killing at the crossroads,
The ritual slaughter done, I faced
Behind the bull-head mask my beastly other.
The earthquake came. The palace fell.
We met our own conception.

Wife Jocasta mother dead, priestess bride deserted
For holding us to witness her embrace
A god with vine-leaves in his hair
Dancing in ecstasy with death
Till passion tears his limbs asunder
Devouring soil dismembers.
Un-manned we fled her secret knowing
Denied the mystery.

                    Old Oedipus
Let Theseus lead you to the centre.
All exiles end at our beginning
For when earth opens wide her thighs
Takes in her son again
If but the victim goes consenting
Bright Hyacinths will spring from his decay.

Come now
Give way to Dionysus' resurrection.
The ground is shaking.

Rebirth

Held
firm warm sure.
Falling down the screaming tunnel
hard white bright   cold
nothing.

They have dis-membered me
drawn a sharp knife of terror
between my this and that

'Her pain is insupportable
anaesthetise and grapple'

denied to me my sibling's death
and mourning.

I try remembering

unlive the years
uncoil my tight-wound spiral
to the centre
where rolling opposites
unite.

Swimming
my cells recall the sea
leap glide
dance joyously.

I climb our mutual rope of sharing
our give and flow
to curl around my womb-mate brother
until our marriage bed is filled
and I must turn to set him free.

I am remembering

life's lust implacable
a force uncaring her or me
will thrust me forth
despite her cries
my clenched and desperate unbreathing
to flounder birthed upon the shore
exhausted
sobbing.

Flesh recollects at last
my forward back and on and through
the past lives in the present
the future's time is now
darkness   contraction   light
the ever-changing contraries
contained within each other
no lines to cross
no discrete boundaries
between my here and there
process
complete and whole.

My body has re-membered me.

Callanish

Of force first heaved at heaven   the sentinel
Stands   still   forbidding clogged approach
It is a pilgrimage   and meet
Where feet have trod   that souls should ache
At every point   upon the pattern
'Til pains confessed and tears have shriven you
And when the well springs free
These ancient stones will watch you pass
The avenue   between   right hand and left
At the circumference of the cross   pause
Recognise your path   and spiral
Widdershins against the sun   unmake the way
Turn in the circle of their moon-marked faces
A congregation from the past   old witnesses
Acknowledge me   I am the earth   the rock
Look down upon the chamber   descend
Between the doors   the outer and the inner
Into the tomb   beneath   my awe-ful presence
Where   I am   neither he nor she
But union   zygote   first unseparate
Turn round full circle in the womb   and exit
Enter   walk new into the world
Unwind the coil   and leave me   peaceful
Prepared   for your return   the journey home

haiku

Pentlands

path's end at the height
hills beyond hills beyond hills
mist into the light

Reflection

two heads, dark and light
reversed behind the mirror
where shadows stand bright

Geese

wing beat, air sighing
over meadows at twilight
geese homeward flying

Crocus

bright crocus breaks earth
life insists, feeling erupts
dark winter gives birth

Samye Ling stones, Autumn equinox

bed rock wrested free
river held at year's balance
grave-borne to the sea

Daddy

Father I've come to the funeral
but my mother forbids me to mourn
lest we spill generations of unwept tears
and grieve for a childhood of pain.
Father your body is ashes
but in dreams' dusty cellars
your uncremated limbs still stir
resisting re-internment.

Daddy, you're late for the wedding:
I've tried so to reach you, time and again,
but the telephone's made out of cardboard,
the wires are cut off in a tangle,
my mother just stands there, tapping her foot,
there's no way for me to get through.
Daddy, you're late for my wedding:
the colourful crowd has dispersed
and taken the unknown groom,
the soaring white pillars, the beautiful church,
the mosaic of light at the window,
have shrunk to a pitiful hall.
Daddy, you've ruined the wedding,
sauntering too late up the hill:
my fairy-tale dress is in tatters,
you can't give me away, after all.

For over and over the pattern's the same
a woman a man tenderness offered
a boundary crossed over and over
sex and secrets and shame
over and over the circle of pain
of love and betrayal desertion denial
the cycle repeated over and over
and over and over again and again.

My girl may not ride upon Daddy's cock-horse
For Mummy is waiting at Banbury Cross
With a ring on her finger and lead on her toes
To silence my music wherever she goes.

The jigsaw is drawing together
the outline is taking a shape
I'm afraid of the hole in the middle
of finding a piece that fits
I don't want to see it complete.

waking
your large hands holding me
it's just a dream
too hard
I don't believe
you're at my back
it isn't true
you're pressing me
I'll wake
too hard to you
I can't believe
too large
too hard
nightmare
it's true

Daddy, Daddy, how did you abuse me?
Did you bugger me for real?
Or only fuck me up
the old familiar way?
Love me and leave me too soon
sex and secrets and shame?

In the dim of the darkroom together,
you teach me enlargement, exposure,
development, stopping and fixing.

A series of snapshots,
an album of disordered pages.

Memory. Fantasy. Dream.

We're playing a game in the big warm bed,
look how it raises the covers!
But there in the mirror she purses her lips
and stares her disapproval.

Beside your chair, I marvel at the lines
you turn into a caricature, a cat.
She says it's time for dinner.

Your careful fingers peel the plaster
from my wounded tom-boy knees.
My mother waits with disinfectant.

Youthful, naked, potent, male,
a figure in the firelight;
a woman sits, disdainful, frowns;
there is an infant witness,
curious, envious, playful.

I have my very own tickets
to take me to magical lands.
You are pursuing crime.
Outside, you'll hold my hand.

Midnight wordless companions,
we savour our contraband supper,
with Bessie Smith singing the blues.

A toddler puddling in the sand
I feel your bulk behind
your large kind hands
firm on my arms to hold me.
Sensations carried down the years
for present recognition:
delightful, warm, exciting.

Is that Freud's ghost I hear,
chuckling across my shoulder?

> *How should I your true love know*
> *From another one?*

It is time for Isis
to re-member her kin

> *We have done but greenly*
> *Thus hugger-mugger to inter him*

I found the lost piece in my hand
I had held it all along

> *He is dead and gone, Lady*
> *He is dead and gone*

no Bacchic spoils or relic to hymn
but comforter and friend

> *Which bewept to the grave did not go*
> *With true-love showers*

Under a fig in Tuscany
between two olive trees
I buried the last of you

> *At his head a grass-green turf*
> *At his heels a stone*

I mourned beneath the burning sun
and put bright poppies on your grave
for rosemary, pansies and rue

> *He is gone, he is gone*
> *And we cast away moan*
> *Gramercy on his soul!*

Thank you Daddy for the present
for joy and pain and living,
your death a final birthday gift,
a wake I'll go on dancing.
Daddy I've given you away:
I'm ready for the wedding.

Fairy Tale

A fairy-tale hag with cruel apple breast,
You've poisoned and laid me impassive to rest,
Frozen asleep in a coffin of glass,
Locked behind barriers no feeling can pass.
You tell me it's safer surrounded by briars,
That love is a myth and princes are liars;
You're turning the mirror with face to the wall
So no one can tell I'm his fairest of all,
For desire is a Beast that Beauty may wake
And harsh is the price if your spell we dare break.
It's all for my good that you maim me and bind me
Alone in the dark where he cannot find me.

•

A monster mother with Basilisk eyes,
A Gorgon Medusa who petrifies,
Forbids me cry or want or enjoy,
And makes of me an inanimate toy.
I am a doll. I am her game.
I am the object without a name.
Roughly held in Harpy's claws,
An avenging Fury with cannibal jaws.

A Bad Mother, Step-mother, gave the Princess birth,
Along to the christening her God-mothers came:
One blessed her with interest and found her of worth,
The other gave laughter and meaning for her name.
Yet years she languished, waiting in her Tower
For the Good Mother's love and her magical power.

Through my glass-walled coffin comes a clear, lilting voice
That tells me to waken and make my own choice,
For here in the pain of my heart lies the key
Which will open the lock – I can set myself free.
The Good Mother casts a long shadow of hate:
This woman, complete, lets me learn to relate.
She is the God-mother no one invited,
Open and willing to meet me, delighted
By both love and rage, by my joy and my grief,
Granting her truth and a sharp disbelief
That cuts through the briars of fearful defence
To the flame at my centre that needs no pretence.

I have met me the Green Man, mother:
A vine springs forth from his lips
That roots in the earth of his chest.
He is placing his hand on my hips
And his mouth is seeking my breast.
– He is calling me out, my lover.

Ours is the garden to rediscover:
Out of his loins a strong tree grows,
His fingers sing raindrops over my ground,
My sunshine has opened, my fountain o'erflows,
I laugh as I blossom his maypole around.
– I am filled by my Green Man, mother.

The Monster is dead, old mother of mine;
We have outlived her, and now it is time
To recognise distance enables the meeting,
To entertain difference, countenance greeting.
Won't you come at the last then, and join in the feast
To celebrate Beauty at one with her Beast?

re-union

I had not known
how we should meet each other

The gulls are keening in the air
and you hand me a small blue shell
that's ridged uneven with growing,
its inner curve polished and scoured
by the kindly ravaging sea.
Well, I shall bring you primroses
and kiss your morning eyes
and we'll remake our greeting
in a bed of laughter and sun.

I did look forward
to some valuable exchange
but I had not expected
such delight

to find again
this joy.

The Wave

Run with the flood
Ebb when you must
Mount to the moon's call
Dare, flow and trust
This tide has to be
Its force will not break you
Cannot unmake you
For you are the wave
And there is only the sea.

Joy Pitman was born in Bristol on the 3rd of February 1945, and started writing poetry at boarding school when she was thirteen. After a first degree in English & Philosophy and a second in Drama and Theatre Arts, she worked as an English teacher in England and an archivist in the USA. She moved to Scotland in 1973, and her home has been in Edinburgh since 1976.

As a founder-member of Stramullion, the pioneering Scottish feminist publishing co-operative, she was closely involved in the editing and design of such books as Sarah Nelson's *Incest – Fact and Myth* and Ellen Galford's first novel, *Moll Cutpurse*.

She now has a small private practice as a psychotherapist, works as a part-time archivist, and occasionally leads writers' workshops and dream groups.

She has published a number of academic articles on figures in the history of medicine. Her poems have appeared in several Scottish anthologies and magazines, and she has given readings in public and for the radio. This is her first collection.